BEER GAMES

BEER GAMES

An Hachette UK Company
www.hachette.co.uk

Summersdale Publishers Ltd
Part of Octopus Publishing Group Limited
Carmelite House
50 Victoria Embankment
LONDON
EC4Y 0DZ
UK

www.summersdale.com

Printed and bound in Malta

ISBN: 978-1-78685-785-9

Disclaimer: The publisher urges care and caution in the pursuit of any of the activities represented in this book. This book is intended for use by adults only. The publisher cannot accept any responsibility for the result of the use or misuse of this book or any loss, injury or damage caused thereby. Please drink responsibly.

Substantial discounts on bulk quantities of Summersdale books are available to corporations, professional associations and other organizations. For details contact general enquiries: telephone: +44 (0) 1243 771107 or email: enquiries@summersdale.com.

BEER
GAMES

A HILARIOUS COLLECTION OF DRINKING GAMES, CHALLENGES AND DARES

summersdale

INTRODUCTION

Do you, the drinker signified, hereby pledge to get tipsy, rowdy and to have an altogether agreeable evening? Do you swear to charge your glasses, enter into the spirit of games and mete out dares and challenges to all? And do you also vow to make dare-dodgers and challenge-chumps who shy from their duties drink a finger of beer as a penalty for being big spoilsport wet fishes?

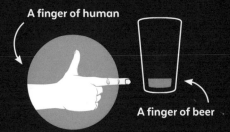

A finger of human

A finger of beer

If the answer is yes, then welcome to the greatest book of drinking games since they took all the fun bits out of the Bible. Gather your pals, crack open a cold one and make yourselves proud.

KEY:

- ◯ A breeze
- ◯◯ Doesn't strain any thinking muscles
- ◯◯◯ A moderate challenge
- ◯◯◯◯ Mo' rules, mo' fun
- ◯◯◯◯◯ Legends only

COUNTDOWN

YOU WILL NEED:

- ★ Two or more players
- ★ Beer
- ★ A clock/watch with a face
- ★ Eyes like a hawk

HOW TO PLAY

Let's start off simple. Each player chooses a number between one and twelve to represent their "slot" on the clock. The game duration is eight minutes, and each time the second hand hits your number you drink a finger of beer. Easy. For some real fun with this game, if you can distract a player into missing their slot then they have to down two fingers.

DRINK OR DARE?

NAME A FAMOUS PERSON THAT EACH MEMBER OF THE GROUP LOOKS LIKE, OR IT'S TWO FINGERS OF BEER. WAIT, WHAT? GOD, NO, DON'T SAY HE LOOKS LIKE *HIM*!

I CHALLENGE YOU TO...

Be the last person in the group
to "break the seal". Or just play it
cool and be the one that causes
a distraction and sneakily wees
in a bottle under the table.

DRINK WHILE YOU THINK

YOU WILL NEED:

* ★ Two or more players
* ★ Beer
* ★ Some grasp of popular culture

Difficulty: O

Players sit in a circle and the first person names a celebrity (e.g. Brad Pitt). The person to their left then names a celebrity whose name begins with the same first letter as that celebrity's last name (e.g. Penélope Cruz). They must drink while they are thinking and can only stop when they suggest a name. And so on, until they run out of beer. Be as quick as you can with your answers, since the more you drink the harder it is to think!

PARANOIA

YOU WILL NEED:

---

* ★ Four or (preferably) more players
* ★ Beer
* ★ Curiosity for idle gossip

HOW TO PLAY

Difficulty: ○

As if it wasn't bad enough that we all talked about you before you got here, now you've got to deal with this. Paranoia is beautifully straightforward: the person to your right whispers a question to you that is answerable with the name of another player (e.g. "Who has the best P.E.-teacher thighs?"). You then answer by saying that name out loud. If that person wants to know what was asked, they have to drink a finger of beer for the knowledge. Top tip: "Who is the most paranoid person playing?" is a great way to land your first sucker. Carry on until the beer runs out.

DRINK OR DARE?

THE TOWERING INFERNAL:
STARRING "YOU" AS A PERSON
TRYING TO BUILD A TOWER TALLER
THAN THEMSELVES THAT STANDS ON
ITS OWN MERIT FOR ONE MINUTE.

I CHALLENGE YOU TO...

Give the birthdays of each of your fellow players. One shot of beer for each special day you don't care enough about to remember.

SIXES

YOU WILL NEED:

* Two or more players
* Beer
* Two dice
* A mind open to the limitless joy of maths

HOW TO PLAY

Difficulty: ◯

Players each take turns to roll the dice. If you happen to roll a six, or two numbers that add up to six (e.g. a two and a four), you drink a finger of beer. Now for the fun stuff: if a player rolls a double, they must drink fingers of beer equivalent to the double they threw (so throwing a double three means three fingers of beer).

As an extra bonus, if a player throws a double six they do EIGHT fingers (one for each six and six for the double!). Rinse and repeat until you're all out of booze.

DIVING QUEEN

YOU WILL NEED:

- ★ Two or more players
- ★ Beer
- ★ A pint glass
- ★ A coin
- ★ Strong wrist action

Difficulty: O

"She was the diving queen/in my drink/really hope she's cleeeeean..." This game has been around as long as there has been money with the Queen's head on it, pint glasses and boredom.

Place the glass in the centre of a table and place your coin half hanging over the edge of said table. Your job is to try to flip the coin into the pint glass. Should you succeed, you can order any one player to drink and then go all mad with power and implement a rule of your choosing. Miss and it's a finger of beer for you. Keep chugging away until you're out of beer, or until your coin rolls under a sofa and you can't get it back. *"He scored the diving queen/made them drink/cos he's super mean, oh yeeeeeah..."*

DRINK OR DARE?

NOMINATE A PLAYER TO BE YOUR SIMON COWELL AND LET THEM CRUSH YOU WITH WITHERING ONE-LINERS FOR A ROUND. "I KNOW THERE'S NO SKILL INVOLVED IN ROLLING DICE, BUT MUST YOU MAKE THAT *QUITE* SO OBVIOUS?"

I CHALLENGE YOU TO...

Drink two fingers of beer from
the same player's glass every
time they leave the room
without being discovered.

BUFFALO

YOU WILL NEED:

★ Two or more players
★ Beer
★ The courage to save a life

Difficulty: ○

Back in the hat-tipping, sarsaparilla-supping West, pistol-toting patrons of the local watering hole could be gunned down and killed if their "shooting hand" was holding a drink. Be the responsible lawman of your turf, and when you see a cowpoke drinking from their dominant hand, call out "buffalo". Any player caught wide-open to attack drinks two fingers of beer. They should then also change hand but, if they don't, that's just more lives to be saving, pardner. Pop a time limit on this one – around thirty minutes should do it.

LADY AND THE TRAMP

YOU WILL NEED:

- ★ Two players
- ★ Beer
- ★ Japanese biscuit sticks
- ★ To be comfortable with invading the personal space of others

HOW TO PLAY

Difficulty: O

The two players place either end of the same biscuit stick in their mouths, and then gradually nibble their way toward each other. The player who chickens out and stops eating first drinks a finger of beer. And if nobody chickens out, well... not to worry. Those dogs in that film seemed to enjoy it.

DRINK OR DARE?

IMAGINE YOUR TONGUE IS A PEN AND SPELL OUT A RUDE WORD IN THE AIR UNTIL THE GROUP CAN GUESS IT. EMBARRASSING? YOU NEVER KNOW WHO YOU'LL IMPRESS.

I CHALLENGE YOU TO...

Clamp a can of beer between your thighs and waddle either three laps of the table or two laps of the room without dropping it.

BAIL OUT

YOU WILL NEED:

★ Two or more players
★ Beer
★ A second empty pint glass
★ Teaspoons
★ A clock/watch with a face
★ Experience of maritime mishaps

Difficulty: ○

Your pedalo has sprung a leak and you're scooping up water in your straw hat and tossing it back in the sea. We've all been there. Thankfully, it'll stand you in good stead to succeed in *Bail Out*.

In this game, you fill one pint glass with beer and leave a second pint glass empty. When the second hand on the clock hits twelve, you have exactly one minute, using your teaspoons, to bail as much beer as you can from the first pint glass into the second. At the end of the minute, any beer remaining in the original glass must be consumed by the furiously bailing individual. So shape up, or ship-out!

IF YOU KNOW WHAT I MEAN

YOU WILL NEED:

★ Three or more players (great with a bit of an audience)

★ Beer

★ To see smut in everything

HOW TO PLAY

Difficulty: ○ ○

Two players are nominated to play and are given a location (e.g. "at a Kwik-Fit store"). They then have a "conversation", trading lines that comically end "if you know what I mean". For example: *"He rolled my spare all over the shop, if you know what I mean."*

The game ends when one player is unable to think of a line or unable to come up with one that, at a stretch, sounds even a bit saucy. That person then drinks two fingers. So have fun, and just go at each other until you're all out of juice – *if you know what I mean.*

DRINK OR DARE?

SIT ON A PLAYER'S LAP?
TSSH. A DARE FOR A PEASANT.
INCONVENIENCE AT LEAST
THREE PLAYERS BY LYING
ACROSS THEIR LAPS, TICKLING
THEIR CHINS AND LAUGHING
FOR THE REST OF THE GAME.

I CHALLENGE YOU TO...

Drink a bottle of beer without the
bottom end of the bottle ever being
higher than level. Did you know you
can get spirit-level apps for phones
now? Just throwing that out there.

JOINED AT THE *BLANK*

YOU WILL NEED:

★ Four or more players
★ Beer
★ Pen and scrap paper
★ A loose attitude toward your *blanks*

Difficulty: O O

Don't you love a game that brings people together? Jot down a selection of body parts, such as right elbow, left foot, bum or forehead, and jumble them up. Pair off into teams of two and ask each member of each team to pick from the pile. Teams must then ensure their chosen areas remain "joined", and must drink two fingers of beer any time they separate. Once you're comfortably connected (if you're lucky), there isn't a lot happening in this one, so top tip: pair off, cosy up and play a *second* game in addition to this one until that lovely golden nectar runs out.

TOP CARD

YOU WILL NEED:

---

* ★ Two or more players
* ★ Beer
* ★ A deck of cards (or several, as each deck serves 6 players)
* ★ Those skills you picked up in Vegas

Difficulty: ○ ○

Players are dealt eight cards, using as many decks as required. The rest of the cards are then placed in the centre of the table to act as the draw pile, and the top card drawn and laid face up next to the stack. The first player lays down cards that add up to the value of the first card, e.g. if the card is a ten, they can play a ten; a seven and a three; or a four, a four and a two.

Cards should be placed on top of the original face up card in any order, determining the next "top card". If the top card can't be matched by the current player, they must drink a finger of beer and pick up two new cards. If the next player matches the new top card using fewer cards than the previous successful player, they can command a different player to drink a finger and choose a player to grab two more cards. Mmm. Lovely power. First person to run out of cards wins.

DRINK OR DARE?

CHOOSE ANY THREE PROPS FROM AROUND THE ROOM AND IMPROVISE A MAGIC TRICK. "I'M GOING TO MAKE MY DIGNITY... DISAPPEAR!"

I CHALLENGE YOU TO...

Choose a buddy and spend a full game plying each other with booze. Blink once for "tilt more", twice for "I'm done", three times for "ah, it's in my lungs".

NUTS AWAY!

- ★ Two or more players
- ★ Beer
- ★ Peanuts
- ★ To not be allergic to peanuts

HOW TO PLAY

Difficulty: ◯ ◯

Each player holds a peanut above their topped-up glasses and (for completely needless tension) holds it there. And holds it. And *holds* it. Then someone calls "Nuts away!" and the peanuts are plopped into your beer. And, behold! Slowly, but surely, those plucky little guys come a-floating back to the top. If your peanut comes last, drink at least half your beer and refill for round two. And then hold it. *Hold* it...

BITE ME

YOU WILL NEED:

* Two or more players
* Beer
* An empty cereal box
* Scissors
* Lovely bendy legs

Difficulty: ⭕ ⭕

While those early-morning squats you've been doing may have turned your bum into mighty mounds of muscle, they've also been training you to be amazing at *Bite Me*.

Cut the "close me" flaps off the top of an empty cereal box and place it upright on the floor in the centre of your group. One by one, with hands behind backs and both feet on the ground, players must manoeuvre themselves so they can pick up the cereal box with their mouth. Once everyone has taken a turn, an inch is cut off the top of the box and everybody goes again. Any player that can't go low enough is out of the game, and must finish their drink.

DRINK OR DARE?

DAMN PAPARAZZI! WHY WON'T THEY LET YOU HAVE A LIFE?! PUT THEM OFF BY PULLING WEIRD FACES EACH TIME YOU TALK, SO THEY CAN'T BE SURE IF IT'S YOU.

I CHALLENGE YOU TO...

Make five unique sounds, each
using a combination of your beer
bottle/glass and your lips. *Fzzzh.*
That's a good one. *Flplplplp.* That's
another. But I'd better stop there.
I've already helped too much.

RETCH-A-SKETCH

YOU WILL NEED:

- ★ Four or more players
- ★ Beer
- ★ Paper and pen
- ★ A timer
- ★ A unique artistic vision

Difficulty: ⭘ ⭘

Budding artist? Accomplished drinker? If you fancy yourself a real "Shandy Warhol" then flex those fingers, sharpen that eye and doodle your mates into dust.

At the beginning of the round, a player whispers a word to the "artist". The timer starts and our maestro begins to draw. Players shout out guesses as to what the picture is meant to be until a correct guess stops the timer and ends the game. The "artist" drinks a finger of beer for every thirty seconds it took to get the answer, while the victorious guesser nominates someone else to drink. Continue until everyone has had a turn. Then everyone leaves happy.

TRUE OR FALSE

YOU WILL NEED:

★ Four or more players
★ Beer
★ Paper and pen
★ A dice
★ To be able to think on your feet

Difficulty: ○ ○

Tear some paper into strips and scribble down either a feeling or an object on each individual piece. Fold them, jumble them up and place them in the centre of the table. Players take it in turns to select a piece of paper from the pile and roll the dice out of the view of the other players. If an odd number is rolled, the player must invent a story about the word; if an even number is rolled, the player must tell a true story.

The other players discuss the story and conclude as a group you're either faithful or fibbing. If they guess right, it's two fingers for you, and if they guess wrong it's two for them.

DRINK OR DARE?

MAKE AN OUTFIT FROM BIN LINERS AND WEAR IT. AND REMEMBER: COCO CHANEL DIDN'T GET TO THE TOP BY PUNCHING A HOLE IN SOME NYLON AND STICKING HER HEAD THROUGH IT.

I CHALLENGE YOU TO...

Impersonate a celebrity until the group can guess who you are. However, "My name is Michael Caine" and famous phrases are not allowed. Some say that'll just lead to terrible, embarrassing impressions. Well, frankly, my dear...

BEER PONG

YOU WILL NEED:

* Two or more players
* Beer
* 16 empty plastic pint cups
* A ping-pong ball
* To live under a rock not to know this

Difficulty: ⚪ ⚪

This is what it's all about. It's Monroe; it's Sinatra; it's Connery. It's an all-time classic. Legend has it that Henry VIII only married so many wives in order to form a team for beer pong.

Combatants stand at either end of a table in front of eight plastic pint cups racked like bowling pins into big triangles (pointing at the other team). Each cup is filled with a different amount of beer. Teams take turns trying to throw the ping-pong ball into their opponents' cups – a successful hit means a member of the opposite team drinks the contents of the cup. Empty cups can be swept aside, or left on the table as a penalty: if the other team throws the ball into an empty, they drink one of their own cups. The game ends when the losing team's cups are either empty or eliminated.

FLIP, SIP OR STRIP

YOU WILL NEED:

- ★ Four or more players
- ★ Beer
- ★ A coin
- ★ To be wearing your good underwear

HOW TO PLAY

Difficulty: ◯ ◯

Players take turns to flip a coin and try to guess the outcome. If the spectators guess right, play moves on. If they guess wrong they each either take a sip of their drink or remove an item of clothing. Play continues until you're all out of beer, or until someone is sitting in their birthday suit.

DRINK OR DARE?

BENJAMIN FRANKLIN FAMOUSLY SAID, "IN THIS WORLD NOTHING CAN BE SAID TO BE CERTAIN, EXCEPT DEATH AND TAXES AND BEING DARED TO IMPROVISE A RAP ABOUT HOW GORGEOUS YOU ARE." LET'S HEAR IT, KANYE.

I CHALLENGE YOU TO...

Tilt your head back, lay an after-dinner mint (one of those fancy chocolate squares) on your forehead and jiggle it down and into your mouth using only the sheer power of your face.

I'M GOING ON A PICNIC

YOU WILL NEED:

* Two or more players
* Beer
* An elaborate memory palace

Difficulty: ◯ ◯

This is the classic memory game, carefully repurposed to get you nice and smashed. Open with the phrase "I'm going on a picnic and I'm bringing..." and then each player contributes to build a list of objects, working their way through the alphabet and recalling all previous answers each time. So, player one might say: "I'm going on a picnic and I'm bringing apples." Player two might then say: "I'm going on a picnic and I'm bringing apples and blue cheese."

On you go until someone messes up, and greatly improves their chances for next time by drinking two fingers of beer. For additional fun, enforce a rule of no repeat answers across rounds. Keep playing until you've had enough, and then just stop. And let's not quibble over who would and wouldn't bring a zoetrope on a picnic. After all, you can only bring that zebra once.

HORSE RACE

YOU WILL NEED:

* Four or more players
* Beer
* A "betting slip"
* A deck of cards
* To commentate like it's the Grand National

Difficulty: ⭘ ⭘

This is probably the closest a card game has ever come to resembling its name. Take the four aces from the pack and place them on the table, face up, in a row. Line eight other random cards, face down, beside the aces, to form an "L" shape. "Punters" choose which "horse" (ace) they think will win, and wager a number of fingers on their betting slip.

When you're ready, turn over the first card. And they're off! The ace that corresponds to the suit of the over-turned card moves ahead to that point and on and on, one by one, up the column, until the final card is flipped and one "horse" wins the race. The losing players sink their wagers, and the winner gets a rosette and a year's supply of ringworm treatment.

DRINK OR DARE?

WITHOUT SPEAKING, PRETEND TO BE A FOOD OF YOUR CHOICE UNTIL THE GROUP CAN GUESS WHAT YOU ARE. DON'T DO DUCK FOIE GRAS POWDERED WITH PISTACHIOS, UNLESS YOU'RE A BLACK BELT IN FOOD-IMITATION.

I CHALLENGE YOU TO...

Flip a plastic pint glass
up and down onto the top
of a 70 cl (24 fl. oz) bottle.

GOON OF FORTUNE

YOU WILL NEED:

- ★ Two or more players
- ★ Beer
- ★ A straw
- ★ A rotary washing line

Difficulty: ○ ○ ○

This game originated in Australia and is named in honour of goon (wine that comes in a kind of plastic bladder) and the TV show of yesteryear, *Wheel of Fortune*.

You hang the goon (or whatever you impressively improvise) on the rotary line, and players stand in a circle around it and give it a good spin. Whoever the beer stops in front of has to drink. You can freestyle too: drink if the line doesn't fully rotate, drink if the goon points toward a tree, etc. And, best of all, the waterfall rule: run in a full circle around the rotary line drinking from the straw until you're back in your original spot. You might not be able to win but, like those spirited contestants on TV, at least you can say you've had a nice day out.

THE TIGER HAS COME

YOU WILL NEED:

* Four or more players
* Beer
* Shot glasses
* A coin
* A large and accommodating table

Difficulty: ○ ○ ○

Don't you just hate it when you're having a drink and a good time and then, suddenly, someone spots a tiger? Seriously, every time.

Players each have a shot glass of beer (separate from their suppin' beverage, pushed near the centre of the table) and generally go about their lives. One person is endowed with the coin. When the person possessing the coin shouts "THE TIGER HAS COME" players have to down their shot and scramble under the table. The last one down drinks two fingers of beer. The coin is then handed to the person on the left, who becomes the new "lookout". Play until everyone has had a turn.

DRINK OR DARE?

SPEND ONE MINUTE DECLARING YOUR SINCEREST, MOST UNDYING LOVE FOR A PLAYER THAT IS *NOT* YOUR SIGNIFICANT OTHER.

I CHALLENGE YOU TO...

Get halfway through your drink and then finish it without using your hands. And no straws either, wise guy.

SHUFFLEBOARD

YOU WILL NEED:

* ★ Four or more players
* ★ Beer
* ★ A large piece of paper and a pen
* ★ A coin

HOW TO PLAY

Difficulty: ○ ○ ○

On a large piece of paper, players write their names and ring them with a tight circle (leaving plenty of space in between circles). Then, each player takes turns to slide a coin down the table so it comes to a stop on the paper. If it stops on a player's name, that player drinks. If it stops in the blank space, you can fill in your own rule, e.g. "everyone drinks", draw a circle around it as big or as small as you like, and continue until you've filled the paper or until your sea legs go completely. And if you miss the board entirely you drink two fingers, because what is the world coming to when your general standard of shuffleboard is *that*?

THE PHOTOGRAPHER

YOU WILL NEED:

- ★ Four or more players
- ★ Beer
- ★ A smartphone
- ★ To spring like a coiled viper

Difficulty: ○ ○ ○

During each game, a different player acts as the "photographer". Their job is to raise their phone, hold it steady, count down from three and take a picture. Anybody not in the frame has to do a finger of beer. They say a photograph is the story of your life without words. Not "without words" in the way you try to describe a drunken night to your mate at 3 a.m. – hunched in an empty bath, over a kebab, murmuring wordless porridge about why you're still single. Classier than that. Play at random throughout the night.

DRINK OR DARE?

ACT LIKE YOU'RE NOT WEARING
TROUSERS OR UNDERWEAR AND
PROTECT YOUR MODESTY FOR
THE NEXT TWO GAMES. USE
EVERYTHING AT YOUR DISPOSAL
TO KEEP THAT FINE-LOOKING
THING CLEAR OF PRYING EYES.

I CHALLENGE YOU TO...

This is like *Grandma's Footsteps*
if grandma was totally wellied.
A nominated player stands beside
a beer at the end of a garden or
long room. Your job is to reach
the beer without being seen.

HEADS UP

YOU WILL NEED:

* Two or more players
* Beer
* A deck of cards

HOW TO PLAY

Difficulty: O O O

Each player is dealt a card and, without looking at what they have, holds it to their head so their fellow players can see its value. After seeing everybody else's card, each player must decide whether to play or fold. Those who say "play" compare cards, with the highest value card declared the winner. If you fold, that's one finger for lacking confidence. If you play and don't score highest, that's two fingers for improper self-belief. And if you have the highest value card, that's a well-done pat on the bum and then straight into round two. The game ends after a solid five rounds.

FRIENDSHIP

YOU WILL NEED:

- ★ Three or more players
- ★ Beer
- ★ A coin
- ★ Eight shot glasses
- ★ "Punishment" ingredients
- ★ Very nice friends

HOW TO PLAY

Difficulty: ◯ ◯ ◯

It's lucky you're all such dear friends because, in this game, you'll need all the mercy you can get. Fill four of the shot glasses with beer, and the other four with "punishment" shots: e.g. hot sauce, pieces of chilli, beer with salt in it. Go nuts. The first player calls the toss and flips a coin. If they're right then, woohoo, it's a shot of refreshing beer for them. If they're wrong, well, they'll be doing a shot but it won't *necessarily* be from the punishments. Their mates get to choose whether it's nasty or nice. Play continues until all shots are gone.

DRINK OR DARE?

TAKE A LEAF FROM MEG RYAN'S BOOK AND FAKE THE BIG "O" LIKE YOU MEAN IT. MAKE THEM WANT WHAT YOU'RE HAVING, YOU SAUCEPOT.

I CHALLENGE YOU TO...

Land a ping-pong ball in a pint glass
after at least two surface bounces.
A star on the Hollywood Walk for
a bounce onto the table, up off a
wall and *then* into the glass.

ON A ROLL

YOU WILL NEED:

* ★ Two or more players
* ★ Beer
* ★ Six plastic cups
* ★ A pen
* ★ A dice

Difficulty: ○ ○ ○

Number your plastic cups from one to six and set them out in a row on the table. The first player rolls the dice and pours their chosen quantity of beer into the cup that corresponds to the dice roll. The next player then rolls: if they roll a different number, they too fill the corresponding cup at their discretion. However, if they roll the same number they drink the contents of that cup and play moves on to the next person. Think long and hard before filling those cups too high, because *On a Roll* is like a box of chocolates: you never know what you're gonna get. Play until you realize what a bad idea it was to start this game. Or until each cup has been filled and drained.

CHEERS TO THE GOVERNOR

YOU WILL NEED:

- ★ Three or more players
- ★ Beer
- ★ To be sober enough to count

HOW TO PLAY

Difficulty: ○ ○ ○

Players sit in a circle, and a random player begins the game by counting "one". The player to their left continues the count, stopping up to three numbers ahead (so they can stop on either "two", "three" of "four"). The next player continues up to three numbers ahead of that, and so on.

The object of the game is to be the player that gets to, say, "twenty-one", because that lucky person gets to enforce a rule. These can be your common-or-garden international drinking rules (no left-hand drinking, no first names to be used for the duration) or they can be specific to each number ("males drink on eight", or "six to ten has to be said in French"). This game keeps going until it collapses under the weight of its own madness. Then you just start over. Cheers to that.

DRINK OR DARE?

RAISE YOUR RIGHT ARM THEATRICALLY AND BEGIN: *"TO BE OR NOT TO BE; THAT IS THE QUESTION."* THEN SPEND TWO MINUTES A.) FINISHING THE SPEECH BEAUTIFULLY OR B.) BLAGGING UNTIL IT'S OVER.

I CHALLENGE YOU TO...

Hold a finger of beer in your mouth and describe your best childhood Christmas gift until the group can guess what it was.

DRUNK STACKING BLOCKS

YOU WILL NEED:

* Two or more players
* Beer
* Stacking block game
* A pen

Difficulty: ○ ○ ○

Write a dare or challenge on each of the fifty-four blocks and build yourself a tight, sturdy tower. Players take turns to "umm" and "ahh" and nudge and poke, and tickle and coax and huff and sigh and *eventually* lever a block from the tower and complete the dare inscribed. Then the block is placed carefully back on top, before the next player "umms" and "ahhs" and so on. Bring the tower down and your drink goes the same way.

For extra fun, build the tower with the dares increasing in difficulty/embarrassment the higher up you go and really challenge those Johnny-pull-from-the-top-ers.

SPIN THE BOTTLE

YOU WILL NEED:

* Four or more players
* Beer
* An empty bottle
* To creep people on the fly

Difficulty: O O O

This is a good one for when your party is already "well on its way". A player spins the bottle. When it lands on another player, look them dead in the eye and say the most bizarrely flirtatious thing your brain gives you. If anybody in the group laughs, they have to drink. But that won't be you, will it, you big box of hot, steaming potatoes? Play until each player has had at least four spins.

DRINK OR DARE?

FOR THE NEXT TEN MINUTES, TURN EVERYTHING YOU SAY INTO A FILTHY INNUENDO. I'M FOREVER TRYING TO GIVE UP MAKING INNUENDOS. WHY IS IT ALWAYS SO HARD?

I CHALLENGE YOU TO...

Drink your next drink using
as many straws as you can
physically suck through.

AROUND THE WORLD

YOU WILL NEED:

- ★ Two or more players
- ★ Beer
- ★ A deck of cards
- ★ A third eye that can see through cards

Difficulty: ○ ○ ○ ○

Pack your suitcase and lotion up because, just as the name suggests, we're going on an all-expenses paid trip to: a game of cards in your house!

A dealer is nominated and play begins when they turn to the player on their left and ask: "Red or black?" The player guesses and a card is dealt. If they're wrong, they drink a finger and play moves on. If they're right, they choose another player to drink. They then play on, making similar guesses with the same penalties for up to four cards. For the second card: is it higher, lower, or the same as the first? For the third card: will the value be inside or outside of the previous two cards? And for the fourth card: which suit will it be? When a player guesses wrong, the game ends and play moves to the next person. Play until you've burned through the entire deck.

DIS/LIKES

YOU WILL NEED:

★ Four or more players
★ Beer
★ Paper and pen
★ Outrageously strong opinions

Difficulty: ○ ○ ○ ○

Each player writes down three of their likes and three of their dislikes on a piece of paper, folds it and then tosses it into a big pile of honesty. One by one, players retrieve a piece of paper and read out what's written on it, with the reader having to guess, for example, who likes the tickly underwater jet at the local pool or who dislikes how dressing room mirrors make them look while they're standing in clothes shops, licking shirts and putting them back on the rails. You guess wrong, you take your medicine. Play ends when all pieces of paper have been read out.

DRINK OR DARE?

YOU'RE A MEMBER OF THE ROYAL FAMILY GOING INTO A CHEMIST TO BUY CONDOMS. FOR ADDED HUMOUR: YOU CAN'T USE THE WORDS "CONDOM", "SHEATH", "RUBBER JOHNNY", "PROPHYLACTIC" OR "LATEX ACTION-SOCK". DREADFULLY INCONVENIENT, WHAT?

I CHALLENGE YOU TO...

Recreate Michelangelo's *The Creation of Adam*. Choose a player to play "God". They will recline, finger outstretched, at the end of the largest room in the house. The player playing "Adam" should spin with their head on a broom, cross the room and meet their outstretched finger *exactly*.

SEVENS

YOU WILL NEED:

★ Three or more players
★ Beer
★ To resist channelling
  Len Goodman – "Se-ven!"

Difficulty: ○ ○ ○ ○

I think we can all agree that the worst thing about leaving school is the scant opportunities afforded by "the real world" to do some lovely maths. You. Are. Welcome.

Players sit in a circle (or whatever shape you like, really – it's your party). The first person says "one", the second says "two", and on it goes as quick as you can. When you hit a multiple of seven (e.g. seven, fourteen, twenty-one) or a number with seven in it (e.g. seventeen, thirty-seven, seventy-one) you shout "NO" instead of saying the number – and the direction of play reverses. Drinking penalties for: saying a number that includes a seven; not realizing play has reversed and missing your number; not realizing play has reversed and saying a number when you shouldn't. Good old maths. Play until you get bored, or until you decide to make a game out of a different cherished school subject.

BLEEDIN' HECK

YOU WILL NEED:

* Two or more players
* Beer
* A dice
* Lady Luck's fair hand

Difficulty: ○ ○ ○ ○

No idea how the title of this game relates to the game itself but, like cats named after people or children named after fruit, it's best to just smile and get on with it.

In Bleedin' Heck a player gets things started by rolling the dice. Everybody else then has three throws to try to match their score. A match is made either by rolling the same number on throw one, or by rolling additional numbers on throw two and (if necessary) throw three, to equal the original throw. If you match the score you're grand; if you go over you drink a finger of beer; and if you go under you drink two fingers, because failing to match one throw with three is some spectacularly hapless work. Play for three full rounds.

DRINK OR DARE?

PUT THE SOCK OF ANOTHER PLAYER ON YOUR HAND AND TALK THROUGH IT FOR THE REST OF THE GAME. IT IS *VERY* IMPORTANT THAT IT DOESN'T HAVE THE SAME VOICE AS YOU.

I CHALLENGE YOU TO...

It appears that, while you were all talking, the floor has become hot lava. Make it from the middle of the room you're in to the middle of a different room without touching the floor.

NEVER HAVE I EVER

YOU WILL NEED:

- ★ Two or more players
- ★ Beer
- ★ NO SHAME

HOW TO PLAY

Difficulty: ○ ○ ○ ○

Players take turns to make a statement informing the group of something they have never done, opening each time with the phrase "Never Have I Ever..." If anybody in attendance has done it, they drink a finger of beer. So an all-round good egg might say: "Never have I ever been on a first date and forgotten the other person's name." And then all your terrible, terrible friends who have done that take a drink. And if you know somebody has done something that you feel the rest of the group should never know, obviously don't say that. Because you're an all-round good egg, remember? Play until each player has made three statements, or until you can no longer bear to make eye contact with each other.

BOTHER MY NEIGHBOUR

YOU WILL NEED:

- ★ Four or more players
- ★ Beer
- ★ A deck of cards
- ★ Some friends (or actors prepared to pretend)

HOW TO PLAY

Difficulty: ○ ○ ○ ○

If you're looking at the word "neighbour" and picturing the inconvenience of movement and social interaction, fear not. Your "neighbour" is just the person beside you, so we can all let old Mr Johnson at number twelve get his head down in peace (if you know what I mean).

You can't really win this game as such, but you can lose by being the player holding the lowest value card when the game ends (note: ace is low for this one). Players are dealt one card and, moving in a circle starting at the dealer's left, decide whether to hold the card they've got or swap it with the neighbour to their left. This continues round back to the dealer, who can either choose to stick or to swap their card with the top card of the deck. Players then turn over their cards, and the one with the lowest value card drinks two fingers. Play for five rounds or, if you're feeling especially neighbourly, go on a little longer.

DRINK OR DARE?

REMEMBER THAT FIRST AWKWARD TIME YOUR PARENTS TOLD YOU ABOUT THE BIRDS AND THE BEES? GIVE A TWO-MINUTE LECTURE TO THE GROUP ON HOW TO HAVE SAFE SEX.

I CHALLENGE YOU TO...

Drink a beer without bending your arm. Epic mode available: if you spill any you have to lick it up.

CONFIDENCE

YOU WILL NEED:

* Three or more players
* Beer
* A coin
* An empty glass

HOW TO PLAY

Difficulty: ○ ○ ○ ○

The first player takes the coin while a second player to their left pours an amount of their beer into the empty glass. This can be as much or as little as the player decides, depending how "confident" they feel that they'll be right. The second player finishes pouring and calls heads or tails, and the first player flips. If the second player calls correctly, the play moves on to the player on their left for them to add to whatever is in the glass. If the second player was wrong, they drain their own amount from the glass and player one flips for them again. This game used to be called "Arrogance", but they do say "Confidence" breeds success. Play until each player has flipped three times.

DON'T SINK

YOU WILL NEED:

- ★ Two or more players
- ★ Beer
- ★ A shot glass
- ★ A spare glass of beer

Difficulty: ○ ○ ○ ○

Lower an empty shot glass into the communal beer so that it bobs safely on top. Players then take turns adding small amounts of their own beer to the shot glass, trying not to sink it. The player that adds that drop too much and causes the glass to go down has to drain the outer glass it tanked in. The question is: play it safe with a smidgen, or slosh it in and sink the next guy? The game ends when seven ships have sunk in your beery seas.

DRINK OR DARE?

YOU KNOW WHEN YOU'RE *REALLY* DANCING AND YOU'RE SO IN THE GROOVE YOU DON'T EVEN NEED A BEAT? GREAT! DANCE FOR ONE MINUTE WITH NO MUSIC, AND LET EVERYBODY PRESENT POST IT ON SOCIAL MEDIA.

I CHALLENGE YOU TO...

Crush a beer can without using your feet. Bonus points if you can do it without looking like a chimp trying to crack a nutshell with a rock.

BOOZY SNAKES AND LADDERS

YOU WILL NEED:

- ★ Two or more players
- ★ Beer
- ★ Snakes and Ladders

Difficulty: ○ ○ ○ ○

Salt and pepper, pins and needles, socks and sandals. Some things are destined to be together. And when parents look at their kids running around and having a great time and say "They go together like beer and Snakes and Ladders", well, this is where the phrase was born.

This is a great game for the "middle" part of your night, where your mates want something simple and they're relaxed enough to consider a game for five-year-olds. Land on a ladder, and up you go while everyone else drinks two fingers. Slip down a snake and it's two fingers for you. Unless, of course, it's that really big snake. Then you need to empty your glass.

FUZZY DUCK

YOU WILL NEED:

* ★ Two or more players
* ★ Beer
* ★ An empty pint glass
* ★ To not mind a bit of naughty language

HOW TO PLAY

Difficulty: ○ ○ ○ ○

Players sit in a circle, with the empty glass in the middle. One player starts the game by saying "fuzzy duck". The player to their left then says "ducky fuzz". On this goes around the circle, with players trying to avoid saying anything that would make Reverend Jones cross his chest and dash you with holy water. And if something unpleasant slips out? The empty glass in the centre is your "swear jar". Each time you say "that which must not be named", a finger of beer goes into the glass. When you're up to five, think hard: next one to swear downs it. Play until the swear jar has been filled and emptied five times.

DRINK OR DARE?

REMEMBER WHEN ALADDIN WISHED TO BE THE OPPOSITE SEX FOR A DAY? NO? HMM. ANYWAY, IT'S WISH GRANTED FOR YOU: ACT OUT WHAT YOU'D DO IF YOU WERE TURNED INTO THE OPPOSITE SEX.

I CHALLENGE YOU TO...

Drink fifteen shots of beer
in the next fifteen minutes.
The quarter-hour of power.

BATTLESHOTS

YOU WILL NEED:

- ★ Two or more players
- ★ Beer
- ★ Paper and pen
- ★ Six shots of beer

HOW TO PLAY

Difficulty: ○ ○ ○ ○ ○

Draw two grids (one each), five squares by five squares, labelling the columns alphabetically and the rows numerically. Hidden from your opponent, scribble Xs in three random boxes of your grid: one X represents your submarine, two Xs your destroyer, and three Xs marks your battleship. Then assign the six shots of beer (three each) to the Xs.

Players take turns to call out grid references, e.g. "A1", trying to sink their foe's fleet. Each "direct hit" requires the drinking of one of the shots on your "X". The game ends when you've hit all three "boats", and the losing captain drinks all remaining shots and respectfully goes down with his ship.

THE WORLD'S CRATE-EST

YOU WILL NEED:

* ★ Two or more players
* ★ Beer
* ★ A crate for each player
* ★ Three miles of track (yes, really)

Difficulty: ○ ○ ○ ○ ○

This one is last because it is, frankly, the Olympics of drinking games. It is not for: the faint of heart, the weak of spirit, those who have spun around twenty times with their head on the tip of a broom for failing at something else. It is for: heroes, legends, gods.

Players place between eight and twelve small bottles of beer in a crate and race each other across the three miles to the finish-line. The catch? Your crate must only contain empty bottles when you cross it. What do you do: drink at the beginning and then peddle those pins, or get a head-start and then chug as you charge? See you on the podium, champ.

If you're interested in finding out more about our books, find us on Facebook at Summersdale Publishers and follow us on Twitter at @Summersdale.

www.summersdale.com

Image credits